How to

Faster

Beginner's Guide to Increasing Your Running Speed and Transforming Your Body With Sprint Training

By Francis Cantrell

Contents

Thank you for buying this book and I hope that you will find it useful. If you will want to share your thoughts on this book, you can do so by leaving a review on the Amazon page, it helps me out a lot.

Introduction

Hi and welcome to this brief, beginners guide to enhancing your running speed and additionally changing your body with sprint training. Running is an exceptional kind of physical exercise, whether you are proactively training for contests, playing social or competitive sports or just utilizing it as part of your cardiovascular regimen. To start this guide, we're going to devote a couple of minutes talking about what sprinting is-- and isn't-- and additionally have a look at the history of sprinting.

What is Sprinting?

Sprinting is a competitive running occasion that is 400 meters or less. A lot of sprinting occasions are 100, 200, or 400 meters. The majority of them last less than one minute due to the fact that sprinters are running as quick as they can throughout the whole length of the race. Some sprinting contests consist of relay races that consist of 4 runners each running a specific range. Sprints in a training sense can additionally indicate doing a specific cardio workout with full-scale extreme anaerobic effort for a quick duration followed by rest.

Sprinting VS Running

Although running and sprinting utilize the identical muscle groups and are basically the identical thing, there are some crucial distinctions. Sprinting, as pointed out previously, consists of professional athletes moving as quickly as they can for the entire sprint in an anaerobic environment, making it far more extreme than running. From a metabolic viewpoint, that indicates you're utilizing glycogen instead of oxygen for your muscles, which uses you out a great deal quicker than a well-paced run.

Running, however, is slower and less extreme than sprinting, so occasions are a lot longer and necessitate physical fitness. Running contests consist of the 5k (3 miles), the 10k (6.3 miles), half-marathons (13 miles), and complete marathons (26.3 miles). Running utilizes oxygen to keep you going, so you can preserve your speed for longer, which is why you need to run for a minimum of 10 minutes for it to be taken into consideration as a workout.

Origin of Sprinting

Sprinting goes back further than any other competitive sport. As a matter of fact, it was the initial kind of athletic contest. The earliest record originated from the initial Olympic Games (776 B.C.). Some specialists think that sprinting might have been the only contest at the first Olympics. During that time, the race was a single stade in length, which is approximately 200 meters.

Contemporary Olympics

When the contemporary Olympics were established in 1896, they consisted of 2 sprinting occasions: 400 meters and 100 meters. Then, in 1900, the 200-meter dash was included. Relay races were featured beginning in 1912 with the 4 x 400 race and the 4 x 100 race. During that time, just males were permitted to contend in the Olympics, however, when females were featured in 1928, sprinting events were on the list.

Advantages of Sprinting

There are lots of advantages to sprinting. It can boost your heart rate and capability to work out. Sprinting additionally burns a big quantity of calories in a brief quantity of time and can enhance your metabolic process, making it a terrific method to drop weight and change your body structure without needing to have to devote hours on a treadmill. Some individuals utilize sprinting as part of a weight-training program since it utilizes a large group of muscles at one time and assists in enhancing them.

Well, that's a short introduction into sprint training and what we'll be covering in this manual. In the following chapters, we're going to concentrate on the various elements of sprinting and assist you in establishing a strategy to get the most out of each sprint session. Are you prepared to start? Let's dive in!

Chapter 1-- Why Are Some Individuals Quicker Than Others?

When you consider exceptional sprinters, you most likely think about Usain Bolt. However, what makes him a lot faster than the typical individual? Definitely, there's more to it than an excellent training regimen. In this part of the course, we will take a more detailed look at how an individual's genes and physical build play into how quick of a runner they are.

Muscle Fibers

What kind of muscle fibers you have is going to incline you to be a greater sprinter, long-distance runner, or leave you someplace in the center. Marathon runners tend to have a greater percentage of slow-twitch fibers that enable them to go the distance. Sprinters typically have more fast-twitch fibers that enable them to go quicker for much shorter time periods.

The typical individual is born with quite an even mix of these 2 muscle types. Nevertheless, there is some proof that demonstrates that you can get approximately 10 percent of these to change by thoroughly training them, so even if you weren't amongst the few talented sprinters that were created with more fast-twitch muscle fibers, you are able to still train to get a couple of more in your corner.

Lactate Threshold

This describes just how much lactate you can take prior to needing to decelerate. Lactate is a natural waste product of muscles as they're working, especially if they're operating in an anaerobic state like when you're running. A greater threshold suggests having the ability to run quicker along with having the ability to keep that quicker speed for longer, which is essential when you are performing at full speed. Luckily, sprinting training assists in boosting this lactate threshold.

Physical Type

This has a little less to do with genes and more to do with your general physical state. Certainly, if you're lugging a couple of additional pounds, you won't have the ability to move as rapidly as somebody who's not. This applies to muscle weight too, which is why the majority of the sprinters you see are lean without much muscle mass to slow them down.

Form

Essential points in your general form consist of how your foot strikes the pavement, how long your strides are, and how well-maintained your gait is. All of these things combined comprise your form. As you refine your form through continued workouts, you are going to end up being a much better, quicker, and more effective sprinter. While some individuals naturally have superior form, it could be acquired through practice.

VO2 Max

This is one thing that numerous middle-distance and long-distance runners are interested in. It determines the maximum volume of oxygen that your body is able to process throughout the workout. Nevertheless, due to the fact that sprinting does not utilize oxygen for sustaining your muscles, this is one thing that doesn't matter that much to sprinters when contrasted to other runners. We discuss it here just due to the fact that it is one thing frequently talked about amongst runners, although it does not actually apply to sprinters.

Despite the fact that you might not have the genes to trump Usain Bolt, you can work to enhance all of these things to make you a much better sprinter in general.

Chapter 2-- What to Do Prior To Starting a Sprint Training Program

You never ever wish to simply leap right into a brand-new workout program, specifically one that is as extensive as sprint training. In this part of the book, we're going to take a look at some things you ought to do prior to beginning with your sprint training to ensure that you lessen your danger of injury and optimize your outcomes as soon as you begin your sprint training program.

1. See Your Physician

The first thing you wish to do is visit your routine physician and discuss your intention to start a sprint training program. Your physician is going to likely wish to analyze you to make certain that you are sufficiently healthy to do this kind of training. Depending upon your age and total fitness level, you might have to have your lungs and heart inspected.

If your medical professional states that you aren't sufficiently healthy to start a sprint training program, listen to them. There are lots of other kinds of workout that you may do to get in shape. You might additionally merely have to get into much better shape by losing some weight and developing some muscle tone prior to starting, so be patient if that holds true.

2. Know Why You're Doing It

Sprint training is tough, so prior to you starting, you wish to make certain you understand why you're doing it. This is going to assist you to remain focused throughout training due to the fact that you have a particular objective in mind. Possibly you're seeking to improve your weight-loss by including some more extensive cardio into your regimen, or you wish to contend in sprinting contests. Whatever it is, keep that objective in your thoughts while training.

3. Research

This sprinting training program is an outstanding way to begin due to the fact that it provides you all of the details you require to understand how to start training as a sprinter. However, do not let your research end here. You ought to additionally view videos of Olympic sprinters to have an excellent understanding of how their bodies move whilst they are running. In case you know anybody who sprints, inquire about it too.

4. Have a Training Routine

Among the very best methods to keep yourself on track with your training is to establish a training regimen. Make sure you offer yourself sufficient time throughout every session to prepare, train, and after that, cool off. All 3 of these are essential to any workout program, specifically one as extensive as sprint training.

The most crucial thing is to choose a time of day that is going to work ideally for you.

You will not be sprinting daily, so prepare your regimen appropriately. Some days, you'll be doing less-intensive workouts to enhance your form, and other days you'll be concentrating on developing particular muscles via strength training. These different workouts are going to need to be spread throughout the week so you do not strain yourself. When you have actually followed all of these guidelines, you'll be prepared to start your sprint training.

Chapter 3-- Fitting Sprinting into a Program

If you currently have a physical fitness program in place, including sprints, you are going to offer a variety of advantages for you. It is going to assist you to develop your lean muscle mass, lose more body fat by improving the metabolic process, along with ehancing your endurance. In this part of the program, you are going to see how you can include sprinting into your present physical fitness program.

Where Can You Sprint?

It is necessary to discover an excellent location to sprint due to the fact that unlike jogging, you're not going to have a great deal of time to think about navigating obstacles should one all of a sudden show up in your course. Make certain no matter where you sprint, it has excellent footing and you will not be stressing over interruptions or distractions. Due to the magnitude of sprinting, an unexpected turn or stop can result in injury.

Some individuals suggest running uphill, however, if you're simply starting, you are going to most likely do better on a flat surface area, and can then discover a sloped surface to boost the intensity later on. It's additionally not suggested to utilize a treadmill due to how difficult it is to manage the speed when you're going that quick, and the quicker you go on a treadmill, the higher the danger of injury.

How Frequently to Sprint

Because of how tough sprinting is on your body, you should not do it more frequently than 2 or 3 times a week. If you are young, fit and healthy, you can attempt for 3 days, however, if your body takes a while to recuperate for different reasons, you ought to just run 2 days a week to avoid overexerting yourself. To enhance your sprinting, you ought to additionally incorporate other muscle-building workouts into the remainder of the week.

Warm-Up

Every exercise session ought to start with a warmup, and it's a lot more crucial when you're including sprints to the mix.

Running utilizes your muscles at practically complete capability, and if you do not put in the time to warm up initially, then you're considerably boosting your danger of straining or tearing something. Depending upon the kind of workouts you usually do, you might need to include some additional warmups prior to sprinting.

Some excellent warmup exercises to incorporate prior to a running workout consist of knee-highs, jumping jacks, side shuffles, and butt-kicks. There are numerous others you can utilize, however, these are going to provide you an idea of the high-energy kinds of warmups that are going to prep your muscles and body to run without injury. Ensure you warm up for 5 to 10 minutes prior to starting.

Cool off

After your sprint, it is similarly essential that you cool off, which implies extending the muscles that you utilized and enabling the muscles to unwind gradually. You'll additionally wish to make certain you're providing your body some time to recuperate throughout the exercise, so you're not simply going hard the whole time. The point of sprinting is to force your body to work, however, you do not wish to force too much too quickly.

As you continue through our sprinting training course, you'll discover much more in-depth info on sprinting training regimens, so keep checking out!

Chapter 4-- Easy Ways to Enhance Your Sprinting

The easiest method to enhance your sprinting when you are simply starting is to focus on your form. If you do not develop a good form early on, then you are going to lose time attempting to fix your form and place yourself at a greater threat for injury. That's why this part of the course will concentrate on the correct sprinting form.

Preparation

All the things in your body ought to be facing forward. That suggests your shoulders, feet and hips ought to all be pointing towards the finishing line. Your eyes, too, ought to be looking ahead and seeing the track approximately 10 meters ahead. Get ready to engage your core muscles for included power by stiffening your stomach muscles and pulling your tummy button inward.

Your upper body involving your jaw, shoulders and neck ought to be unwinded, so take a deep breath prior to running and deliberately unwind these muscles. In case you are squeezing them as you run, you are going to make your body work harder than required in these spots, taking energy from other muscles.

Presuming the correct standing beginning position is as simple as moving your dominant leg back a little while keeping the majority of your weight on your non-dominant leg that is at the beginning line. Then, flex your knees a bit as you flex somewhat at the waist. Your arms ought to likewise remain in position, with your non-dominant arm back and your dominant arm forward.

Appropriate Sprinting Form

Begin by pushing off with your front leg, utilizing your toes to propel yourself onward. From there, every stride ought to look identical.

Your dominant leg ought to extend to the outside up until your knee is at the identical level as your hip. Your ankle and knee ought to be at a 90-degree angle. Your other arm ought to be back and kept angled at a 90-degree angle. Then, you'll utilize your dominant leg to move yourself forward and get your non-dominant leg into an identical position and continue up until you get to the goal.

As you run, you are going to additionally require your arms to move in sync with your legs to boost speed. Maintain your elbows angled at 90-degree angles, your shoulders and hands unwinded, and move your hands in tempo with your knees, from your hip up to your chin. When every foot strikes the ground, you wish to land initially with your heel, then roll your foot ahead to propel yourself from your toe as you did on your initial stride. Having powerful, strong foot-falls is among the most fundamental parts of having the ability to boost your running speed.

Practicing the Form

The very best method to practice your form is throughout your warmup due to the fact that it's a lot simpler to keep everything in mind when you're moving more slowly. If you're not working with a coach or an experienced sprinter, then you might gain from filming yourself and examining the videos to see how well you did and what you have to work on. There are additional tools that can assist, which are going to be talked about later on in the program.

Chapter 5-- Standard Sprint Training Regimen for Novices

When you initially get started with sprint training, you are going to just have the ability to run for 2 days a week due to the high level of severity involved with sprinting. Nevertheless, as your body enhances and can deal with more, you might have the ability to move up to 3 days weekly. On those days, you are going to wish to carefully follow this sprint training regimen for novices.

1. Warm Up

Prior to pushing your muscles to the max, you have to get them all set by warming up. There are a variety of warmups that you may do to get ready to sprint, so you can switch out a few of these for comparable activities to match your requirements and inclinations. What is necessary is that you make an effort to warm up prior to starting.

- Quickly jog or walk for 10 minutes. In case you are on a track, go around two times. Make certain to be working at your sprinting form as much as feasible throughout this.

- Locate a vertical surface area to do forward and sideways wall swings. You'll wish to do a minimum of 10 of each with each of your legs.

- Perform high knees by running in spot for a minute while getting your knees up as high as you can.

- Perform butt kicks by running in spot for a minute while at the same time kicking your butt with your heels.

- Round off with some bodyweight lunges for approximately a minute for every leg.

2. Interval Training

Sprint training needs to be done via interval training, which implies you alter your speed and work out in intervals, instead of merely going hard for the whole training session. It is necessary to provide your body the time to recuperate and rest in between sprints. We will offer you 2 methods to separate this part of the training into intervals, one based upon time and the other on the range.

Approach 1: Range

Keep in mind: this approach works ideally if you are utilizing a basic 400-meter track to train on.

- Sprint for 400 meters (1 total lap).

- Go slowly for 400 meters.

- Sprint for 200 meters.

- Go slowly for 200 meters.

- Sprint for 100 meters.

- Go slowly for 100 meters.

Approach 2: Time

- Sprint for 90 seconds.

- Walk for 90 seconds.

- Sprint for 60 seconds.

- Walk for 60 seconds.

- Sprint for 30 seconds.

- Walk for 30 seconds.

3. Cool off

Similarly essential as the warming up, cooling off effectively is going to assist your muscles to unwind so that you don't end up being tense or knotted. There are a lot of stretches you may do for each of the primary muscle groups you are going to be dealing with, so select a couple for every group that work effectively for you and perform those throughout each of these parts of the cool off.

- Gradually jog or walk quickly for 15 minutes.

- Stretch your quads.

- Stretch your hamstrings.

- Stretch your calves.

- Stretch your glutes.

- Stretch your abdominals.

- Stretch your abductors.

In the following part of the program, we will focus a lot more on recuperation possibilities for sprint training.

Chapter 6-- Sprint Training Recuperation

In this part, we will expand on some recuperation methods that you may do following a sprint session to enhance your body's capability to recuperate from the extreme exercise that you had. Appropriate recuperation is essential to stay clear of extreme tenderness and is going to enable your body to build up the appropriate muscles to enhance your capability to sprint. There are 3 primary elements of recuperation that we will cover.

Water

Remaining hydrated is vital for all of your body's functions, and is specifically essential when your body is losing additional water through sweat and working more than usual. Stay clear of consuming a great deal of water prior to your exercise since you do not want it sloshing around your stomach as you run, however, make certain to consume a minimum of 3 glasses of water within an hour after your exercise, then carry on drinking for the remainder of the day.

Nutrition

In case you're not providing your body what it requires to grow your muscles and recuperate from a rigorous exercise, you're going to find yourself having a hard time day in day out. If you desire your body to be as healthy as conceivable, you can't do it with workout alone, so if you have not currently made modifications to your diet plan to enhance your health, it's time to begin.

Quickly after your exercise, you wish to offer your body a large dosage of protein and a couple of simple sugars. Protein is what your muscles are going to utilize to fix the damage you did throughout the exercise and make your muscles sturdier. Simple sugars are necessary since you have most likely burned through what you had in your body prior. Getting a protein shake with a bit of fruit is the ideal post-workout treat.

About an hour after your exercising, you'll wish to consume a great meal that consists of more lean protein, some healthy fats, and a great deal of veggies. Getting lots of veggies is going to offer you some more great carbs that your body can utilize, however, it additionally supplies you with a lot of anti-oxidants, which assist get rid of the waste your muscles burned throughout the exercise.

Sleep

You wish to make certain that you're getting a lot of sleep when you're forcing your body to work hard. If possible, you ought to sleep about 2 hours after your exercise. The timing is essential due to the fact that it's approximately 2 hours after you work out that your body actually begins fixing the muscle damage, so enabling yourself to entirely rest throughout that time is going to assist your body focus completely on healing.

It's additionally essential that you're getting sufficient sleep during the night. The majority of grownups ought to be getting in between 7 and 8 hours of sleep every night. Sprint training and working out generally ought to assist you to feel more worn out at the end of the day, however, if you're still not getting all the sleep you require, there are a variety of methods that you can attempt that are going to assist you in getting a complete night of rest each night.

The bottom line with recuperation is that the more you recuperate, the more you can run the following training day.

Chapter 7-- Running Equipment

Having the appropriate equipment when sprint training is going to assist you in running quicker and preventing injury, however, having the incorrect equipment is going to slow you down and can, in fact, trigger injuries. That's why going slowly and choosing the appropriate equipment at the start is so essential to your success as a sprinter. It's additionally why we're putting in the time in this course to talk about the equipment that you'll require.

Running Spikes

These are the most vital part of your sprinting equipment, so we will devote the greatest amount of time talking about them. Spikes are unique running shoes that are developed for numerous field and track events, so you have to search for one that is made particularly for the range you'll be running. You ought to have the ability to locate what you require at sports or running specialty shop.

Spikes supply traction in between you and the floor right where you require it. In sprinting, all the spikes are on the frontal part of your foot to permit you to clasp the track and plunge yourself forward with each stride. They have a great deal of spikes contrasted to other running shoes and seldom have any in the heel part of the foot because you do not require them there.

Try out a couple of sets prior to picking what you purchase. A lot of sprinters choose to have their spikes tight, contrasted to other kinds of training shoes. Some even get spikes a complete size tinier than their other running shoes. Although it is your choice, remember that as you're running quickly, you wish for your shoes to be with you 100% and not have any looseness.

These are going to simply be your greatest financial investment when it concerns running equipment. While high-end spikes are going to easily cost you $100 or more, you can normally locate a good set for approximately $50. Nevertheless, these shoes ought to last you for numerous years, and that makes them well worth the financial investment, even if you need to change a few of the spikes along the road.

Running Shorts

The most essential aspect of running shorts for sprinting is that they are made from components that are breathable, comfy, and versatile. For training, that's actually the only thing that matters. For racing, you are going to typically desire something that is form-fitting in order to restrict your wind resistance. If you are intending on running in contests, it's a great idea to additionally practice in your racing clothes.

Running T-shirts

Everything that applies to running shorts additionally applies to t-shirts. The most significant thing to bear in mind when picking a t-shirt for running is that you wish to ensure you have the ability to move your shoulders easily. This is why you see numerous Olympic professional athletes utilizing sleeveless uniforms or vests.

Warmup and Cooldown Clothing

Since spikes are created particularly for running, you do not wish to use them throughout your warmup or cooldown sessions as this is going to make those more difficult and place more tear and wear on your spikes. So, make sure to bring routine training shoes for those times in addition to sweats or other comfy clothing items that you can use prior to and after your sprint training.

Chapter 8-- Plyometric Training

Although the main focus of sprint training ought to be the actual sprinting itself to enhance your form and speed, there are a variety of other workouts that you may do to strengthen the muscles that you utilize to move quickly. That's where plyometric training appears. In this part of the course, we will discuss what plyometric training is, and provide you 3 exercises that are going to assist with your performance.

What is Plyometric Training

Plyometric training is additionally called jump training since it's primary focus is on numerous high-intensity leaping workouts to boost your strength and speed. There are a variety of various workouts that fall under the classification of plyometric training, however, you need to beware which ones you do since some are suggested for strength training, whereas others are going to boost your speed.

When including plyometric workouts into your sprint training regimen, make certain to do these on days that you are not running. This is since these workouts are similarly high-intensity exercises and doing these in addition to sprints in the identical day is too tough on your muscles. You ought to restrict plyometric training to 2 days weekly.

Here are 3 plyometric exercises that are going to assist you to boost your speed:

Forward Bounds

For this activity, you are going to basically be sprinting one stride at once. The objective is to utilize as much force as feasible to move yourself ahead into a long bound. Make certain to utilize the correct sprint form for this drill as you propel yourself off the balls of your foot from one stride to another. This is going to assist you to optimize your power output for each stride you take and can assist you to extend your strides.

Perform 2-3 sets of forward bounds of 21 yards each while enabling yourself a couple of minutes of relaxation in between sets.

Repetitive Standing Long Jumps

This drill is going to assist you to coordinate your lower and upper body, and is going to assist you to reduce the time you spend on the ground that is going to assist you to move quicker down the track. To perform repetitive standing long jumps, start with your feet in accordance with your shoulders, then leap ahead as far as you are able to. Once you feel the ground with the balls of your feet, propel yourself into one more long jump, and so forth.

Perform 3 sets of repetitive standing long jumps of 21 yards each, relaxing for a couple of minutes in between sets.

Depth Jumps to Standing Long Jumps

The object of this plyometric workout is to train your body to naturally take off ahead the moment the balls of your feet reach the ground. To perform a depth jump to standing long jump, begin on a steady surface area that's at minimum 1-foot high. Step off and make certain to land with two feet on the ground, and after that, instantly do a single standing long jump.

Perform 3 sets of 5 depth leaps to standing long jumps along with a couple of minutes of relaxation in between.

Chapter 9-- How Strength Training & Muscle-Building Can Help With Sprinting

In this part of the book, there are a number of reasons why you ought to be integrating strength training and muscle-building workouts into your workout regimen for sprint training. Here are a couple of particular manners in which strength training can assist you to run quicker:

1. More Force

Physics informs us that the higher the force on a thing is, the quicker it is going to move. This is likewise correct when it concerns running. The more force your body has the ability to produce in your leg muscles, the quicker you are going to have the ability to speed up forward. By developing the appropriate leg muscles, you can enhance the quantity of force they have the ability to generate on every stride.

2. Less Mass

Returning to that physics lesson, we additionally understand that the tinier a thing is, the higher the impact of the force that's being placed on it. Strength training assists you in reducing your total mass by burning body fat which is going to assist you have the ability to go quicker with the identical quantity of force. Being lighter on your feet while running is going to additionally assist in keeping you from burning out as rapidly.

3. Decreased Injury Risk

While sprinting, your joints, muscles, tendons and ligaments all need to operate at complete capability. If they are not currently strong, then the pressure of sprinting can result in injury. With strength training, you can develop these fundamental parts in a more concentrated, slow-paced environment to ensure that when you hop on the track, they'll be prepared to work together effectively.

4. Better Balance

Odds are you naturally have one leg that's more powerful than the other. While this will not impact your life, it is going to damage your capability to sprint well and places you at a greater threat of injury when you are out of balance. With strength training, you may do single-arm or single-leg workouts to develop the muscles on the weaker side up until the two sides are harmonized in strength.

5. More Fast-Twitch Muscle Fibers.

As we went over previously in the book, fast-twitch muscle fibers are the ones you desire more of so you are able to run quicker. Even though we still have a lot to uncover about muscle fibers, we do understand that through specific workouts, you can change your ratio of muscle fibers to obtain more fast-twitch. Through strength training, you may do targeted workouts that are going to eventually enhance your running speed.

How to Include Strength Training

Arrange your strength training on days when you're not running, and make certain to concentrate on a different group of muscles each day. You ought to train the most on your core and leg muscles, however, arms ought to additionally be included. If you are brand-new to strength training, ensure you figure out each brand-new exercise and practice it well prior to raising the weight, repetitions, or sets. It is essential to do each motion exactly to prevent injury and to really receive something out of it.

Chapter 10 - Advanced Sprint Workouts

As soon as you get the fundamentals of sprinting down, you'll wish to start to challenge yourself to keep improving. To do that, you'll wish to include some advanced exercises to your regimen. Another method to challenge yourself more is to train with a group. In this part, we'll provide you some sophisticated exercises that you can try out a team and as a person.

Group Sprinting

Whether you just wish to exercise in a group to keep one another answerable and to have more fun or you're training with a group so as to compete, you'll have to do things in a different way compared to when you're exercising alone. Here is a terrific group sprinting regimen that you may follow with your workout pals or colleagues to enhance your sprinting capabilities.

- Warm up as usual.

- Everyone spreads out uniformly along the whole length of the track.

- Everybody starts running at a low speed.

- A single person sprints up until they reach the individual in front of them, then slows to a jog.

- The next individual then runs as much as the individual before them.

- This continues up until everybody has actually sprinted. Depending upon the size of the group, you might have the ability to do numerous of these drills straight, or you might require more time to rest in between sets, however, you ought to attempt to perform this 3 times.

- Cool off as usual.

Advanced Regimen

This regimen is excellent for training on a track as you get advanced. It's particularly excellent if you generally just sprint in straight lines since it teaches you to run effectively on the curves of the track too. It is going to be easier if you have 4 cones or other easy-to-see visual markers at each of the points along the track, however, if not, then you may merely utilize the track itself, which ought to be marked.

- Warm up as usual.

- Put your cones at every corner of the track

- Sprint between cone 1 and cone 2.

- Jog between cone 2 and cone 3.

- Sprint between cone 3 and cone 4.

- Jog between cone 4 and cone 1.

- Stroll one and 1/4th of a lap around the track to recover.

- Sprint between cone 2 and cone 3.

- Jog between cone 3 and cone 4.

- Sprint between cone 4 and cone 1.

- Jog between cone 1 and cone 2.

- Repeat.

- Cool off as usual.

With this regimen, if you begin on a straight side, throughout the initial half you are going to jog the curves and sprint the sides. Then on the 2nd half, you are going to jog the straightaways and sprint the curves. To mix it up additionally, in case you are by yourself on the track, you can do the following set sprinting in the opposite direction.

Conclusion-- Tracking Your Progress

Congrats on making it to the conclusion of this brief guide about boosting your running speed and improving your body with sprint training. You might be shocked to learn that most individuals who begin something never ever complete it.

Take your time and advance at your own rate. The more you comprehend and understand about developing the discipline required to attain the sprinting objectives you set, the better your odds. If you actually wish to be successful, then whatever you do for your life needs to be for the long-term. These modifications you're making are not intended to be short-lived. They're intended to be part of a brand-new way of life that you adhere to.

You can't consider sprint training as just as something that you do here and there. Sprint training needs to rather be something that your life is about, and just then can you really reap the benefits. To conclude this book, we are going to cover tracking your progress with sprinting.

Tracking your progress is a fantastic method to encourage you to keep training when you can see your development and definite numbers, however, utilizing the right tools is going to, in fact, assist you to enhance your sprinting and shave time off of your sprints. In this last portion of the program, you are going to come across a few of the tools you can utilize to monitor your sprint progression.

Trackers

Unless you have actually been living beneath a rock, you've seen or heard about fitness trackers that you don on your hand. They are able to track your heart rate, sleep and even map out where you stroll throughout the day. These are fantastic for assisting you to monitor your total fitness throughout the day, and your heart rate throughout sprint exercises.

Prior to purchasing, ensure the one you get works effectively with high-intensity exercises considering that a number of these are developed for range instead of strength. Physical fitness trackers to try to find are ones that inspect your statistics more frequently. After your sessions, you can sync your gadget with your smartphone or PC to see how well you performed.

Slow-Motion Camera

While this could be a large financial investment, if you're serious about running, you'll desire one to film your sprints so you can see precisely what you are doing. Although you might utilize a routine camera and slow the video down, it's merely not the same as utilizing a high-speed or slow-motion camera to get an in-depth, frame-by-frame look.

Additionally, there is a phone application referred to as Coach's Eye that enables you to utilize your phone's camera to capture your sprint and then thoroughly examine it. This app additionally permits you to share your workouts with other folks to receive feedback from other sprinters to enhance your form. If your phone has an impressive camera, this might be a big advantage to you.

Smart Shoes

Every little thing is becoming smarter in this technologically-driven world, including your shoes. There are a number of shoes on the marketplace now that you can utilize while training that can supply you with all the data you require to enhance your sprinting form. They can show you precisely what part of the foot is striking the ground, just how much weight you're placing on various areas of your feet, and for how long your feet are touching the floor.

The shoes you pick to sprint in can have a big effect on your speed, so ensure you get a set that is going to work for you. Additionally, you can additionally locate socks and insoles that are pressure-sensitive and can supply you with the identical data as smart shoes, however, you can effortlessly use these with your typical spiked sprinting shoes.

Community

An often-overlooked resource that can assist you in tracking your development and enhance your running capabilities is a community with other sprinters and runners. The web is the very best place to get in touch with other sprinters when you have questions about anything, and you can additionally utilize it to locate training partners in your location to team up with.

I hope that you enjoyed reading through this book and that you have found it useful. If you want to share your thoughts on this book, you can do so by leaving a review on the Amazon page. Have a great rest of the day.

Printed in Great Britain
by Amazon

12606551R00037